WITHDRAWN

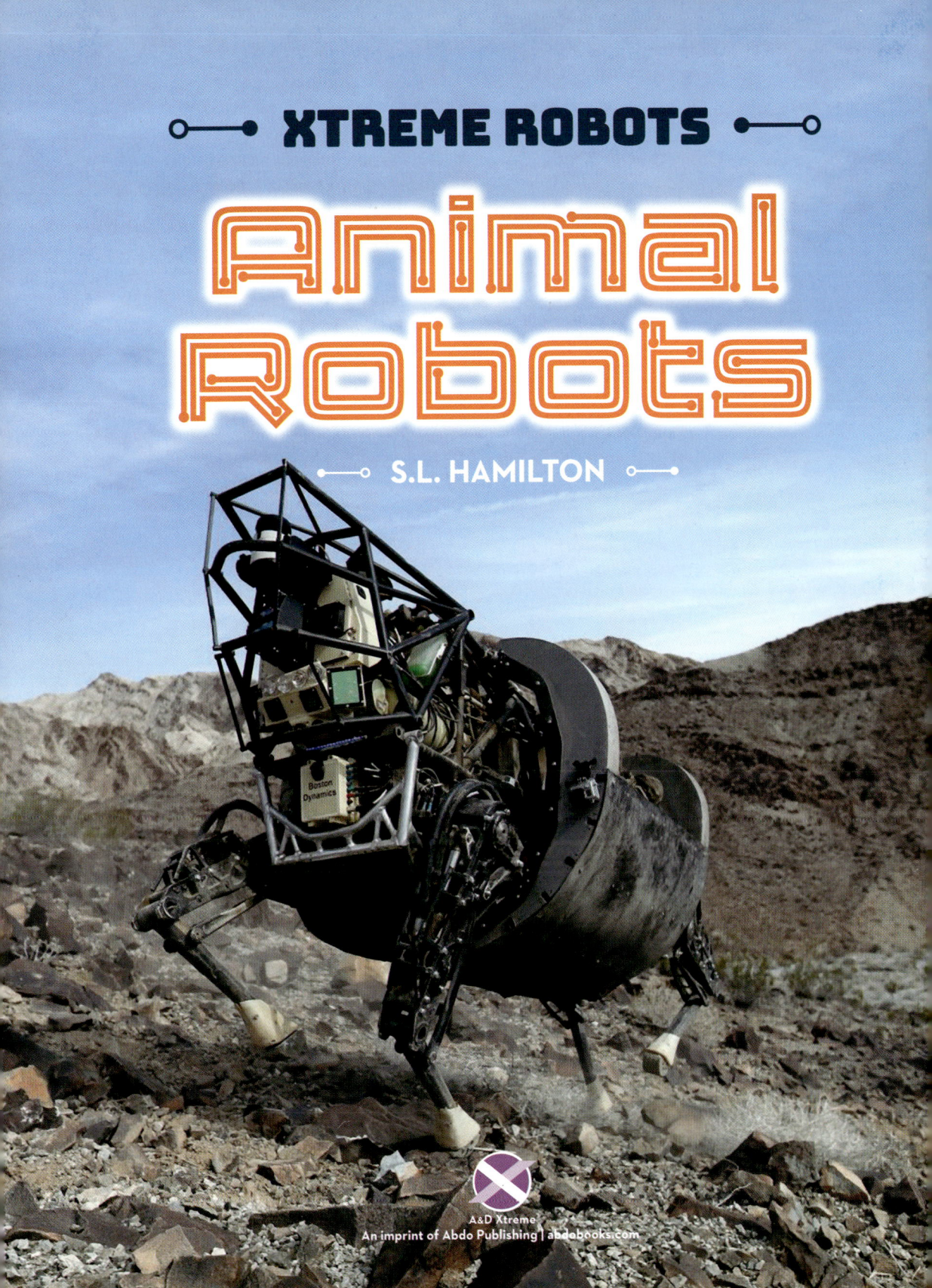

abdobooks.com

Published by Abdo Publishing, a division of ABDO, PO Box 398166, Minneapolis, Minnesota 55439. Copyright ©2019 by Abdo Consulting Group, Inc. International copyrights reserved in all countries. No part of this book may be reproduced in any form without written permission from the publisher. A&D Xtreme™ is a trademark and logo of Abdo Publishing.

Printed in the United States of America, North Mankato, MN.
092018
012019

THIS BOOK CONTAINS RECYCLED MATERIALS

Editor: John Hamilton
Copy Editor: Bridget O'Brien
Graphic Design: Sue Hamilton
Cover Design: Candice Keimig and Pakou Moua
Cover Photo: AP
Interior Photos & Illustrations: AeroVironment-pg 23;
Ageless Innovation-pg 15 (bottom); AP-pgs 6-7, 8-9, 10-11 & 18-19;
Boston Dynamics-pgs 1, 2-3 & 12-13;
EPFL/Konstantinos Karakasiliotis & Robin Thandiackal-pg 28;
Festo Corporation-pgs 20-21, 22, 25, 26 & 30;
iStock-pgs 4-5 & 29 (bottom);
Massachusetts Institute of Technology-pgs 14 & 32;
U.S. Marine Corps-pgs 16 & 17; University of Leeds-pg 29 (top);
University of Washington AIR Lab/Mark Stone-pg 27;
Vincross-pg 24; Yukai Engineering-pg 15 (top).

Library of Congress Control Number: 2018950004
Publisher's Cataloging-in-Publication Data

Names: Hamilton, S.L., author.
Title: Animal robots / by S.L. Hamilton.
Description: Minneapolis, Minnesota : Abdo Publishing, 2019 | Series: Xtreme robots | Includes online resources and index.
Identifiers: ISBN 9781532118227 (lib. bdg.) | ISBN 9781532171406 (ebook)
Subjects: LCSH: Robotic pets--Juvenile literature. | Robots--Juvenile literature. | Technological innovations--Juvenile literature. | Personal robots--Juvenile literature.
Classification: DDC 629.892--dc23

Contents

Animal Robots 4
Dog Robots 6
Wolf Robots 10
Cat Robots 12
Pack Mule Robots 16
Fish Robots 18
Bird Robots 22
Spider Robots 24
Insect Robots 26
Amphibian Robots 28
Glossary 30
Online Resources 31
Index 32

Animal Robots

Robotic dogs, cats, frogs, fish, birds, spiders, and even insects are whirring their way into our lives. Some are designed to be toy pets, while others have jobs to do. Engineers use complex technology to make these robotic animals walk, run, swim, and fly. While difficult to create, animal robots charm their humans.

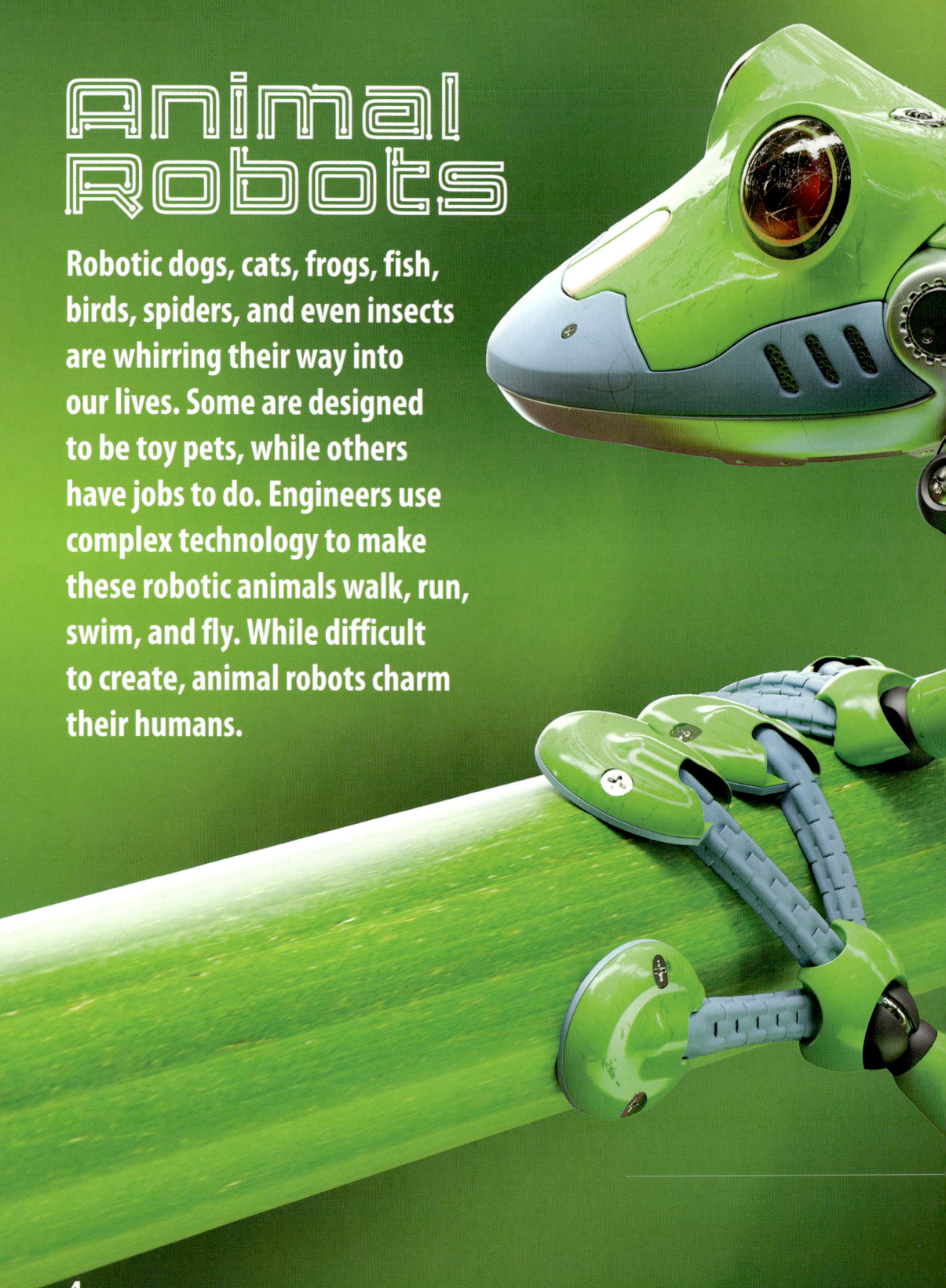

XTREME FACT – When engineers use a life-form in nature to create robots, it is called biomimicry.

Dog Robots

A dog robot is not only a human's best mechanical friend, but also a great worker. Boston Dynamics' SpotMini can pick up objects. It uses its "head," which is really an expandable arm with sensors and cameras. This mechanical pup's clever programming allows it to trot alongside a person. If it slips or is pushed, SpotMini can right itself and keep moving. It is a medium-sized "dog," standing 2.75 feet (.84 m) tall and weighing 66 pounds (30 kg). SpotMini is electronic, quiet, and runs for about 90 minutes before it has to be recharged.

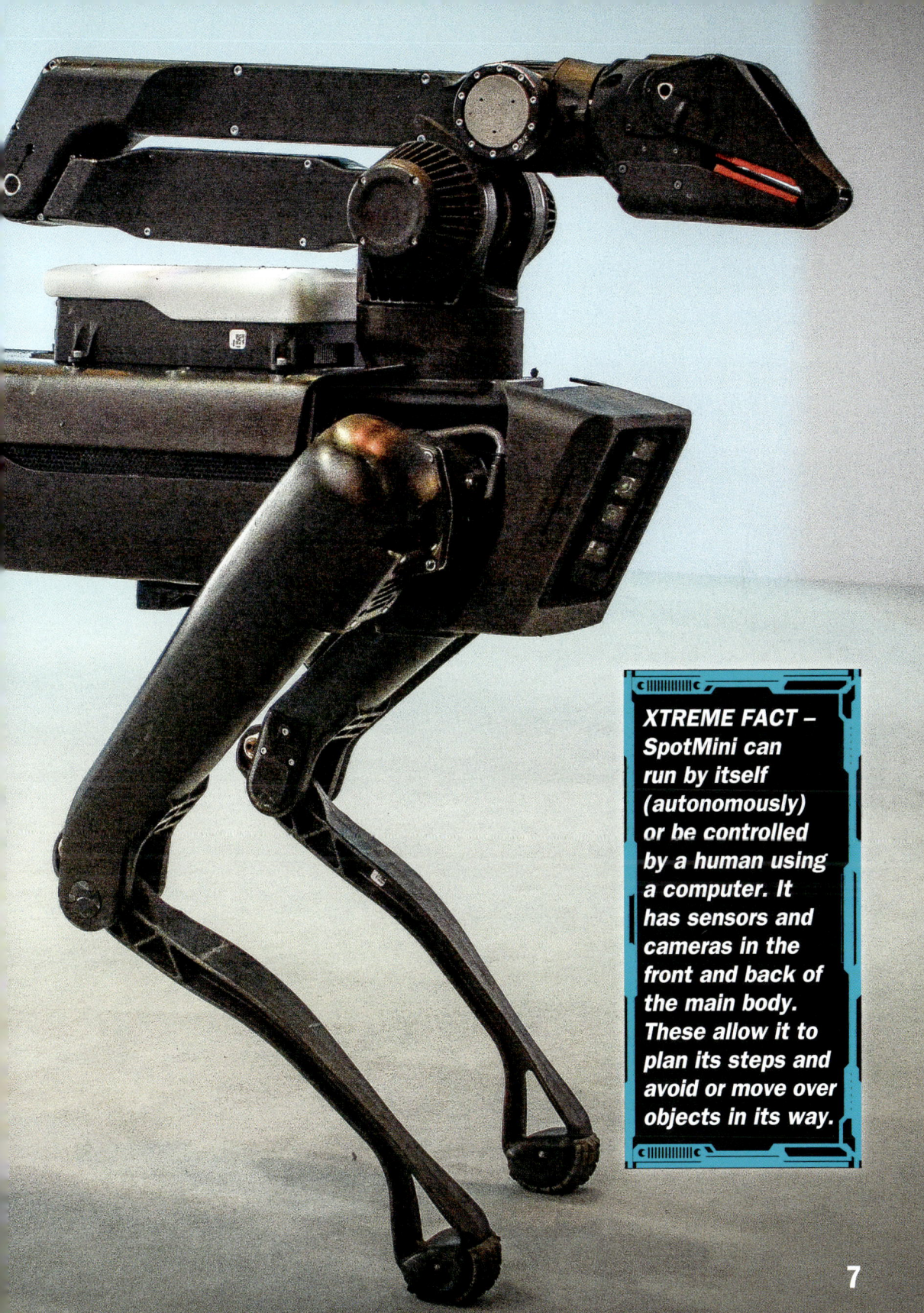

XTREME FACT – SpotMini can run by itself (autonomously) or be controlled by a human using a computer. It has sensors and cameras in the front and back of the main body. These allow it to plan its steps and avoid or move over objects in its way.

Some robotic dogs are designed to be pets. While simpler in design, these robots still require complex programming. Sony's Aibo robotic dog can walk, bark, scratch, and sit. It learns to recognize its owner through cameras in its eyes and nose. These pups have touch-sensitive petting spots on different parts of their bodies that bring happy yips, whines, and tail wags. Some robotic pets are autonomous, which means they can perform tasks by themselves. Many know when they need to "sleep." Like real puppies, they go to their beds to rest and recharge.

XTREME FACT – Sony's Aibo robot dog reacts to human voice commands like sit and high-five.

Wolf Robots

Super Monster Wolf looks scary, but is a great friend to farmers. This solar-powered Japanese robot has blazing red eyes, fierce-looking white teeth, and scruffy fur. Its job is to protect crops. Placed in a field, its glowing motion-detector eye cameras scan the area. When it senses animal movements it howls one of 18 different frightening sounds. These include a human scream and a gunshot. It scares away wild boars and deer from rice, potato, and chestnut crops.

> **XTREME FACT** – Super Monster Wolf acts as a replacement for Japan's natural wolf predators, which were wiped out in the wild in the early 1800s.

Super Monster Wolf

Cat Robots

WildCat is called "the fastest free running quadruped robot in the world." This Boston Dynamics robotic "kitty" runs about 20 miles per hour (32 kph) on flat surfaces. However, it is designed to move over all types of terrain. It uses onboard sensors to keep itself upright while it trots, bounds, and gallops. Its laser rangefinders tell the cat's computers exactly how far away it is from the ground at any one moment. The robot is nearly 4 feet (1.2 m) tall and weighs 340 pounds (154 kg). WildCat's body is surrounded by roll bars and pads for protection if it falls. Its speed may one day be used to carry medical or military supplies.

WildCat

XTREME FACT – WildCat is very noisy! Its combustion engine runs on methanol, a type of liquid alcohol. The "kitty" sounds like a super-loud lawn mower.

Walking is a tough skill for robots. Massachusetts Institute of Technology (MIT) created a robotic cat that not only can walk, but also run, jump, and climb stairs—even with objects in its way. Cheetah moves without camera "eyes." It uses internal sensors to "feel" its way along. It may one day be used to search smoke-filled or unlit areas. This "blind locomotion" will help Cheetah move safely through dangerous situations.

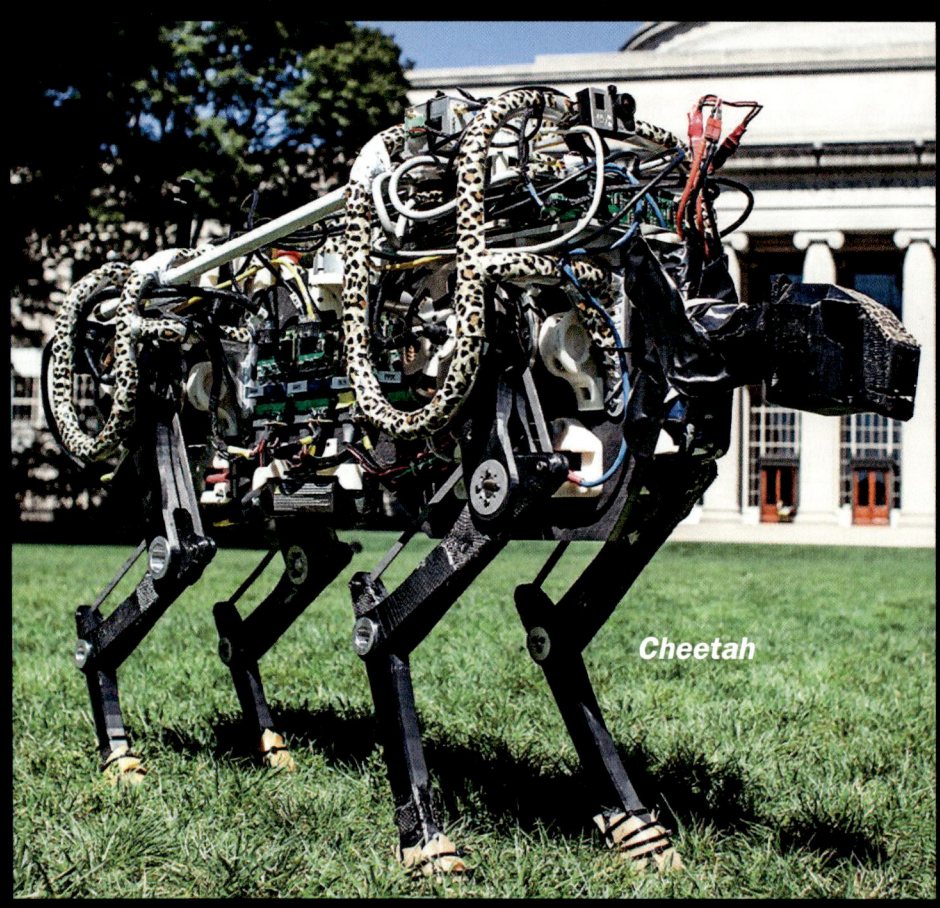

Cheetah

Qoobo is a soft, purring, tail-wagging, catlike cushion.

Robotic cats make good pets for people who can't have a real live kitty. The furry robot friends have proven to make people feel happy. There are no vet bills, food to buy, or litter boxes to empty. People can just enjoy cuddling a soft, purring friend.

Joy For All's companion cat meows and purrs when petted.

Pack Mule Robots

Boston Dynamics has created a robotic pack mule known as LS3 (Legged Squad Support System), or "BigDog." It is called the first advanced rough-terrain robot. BigDog stands 3.3 feet (1 m) tall and weighs 240 pounds (109 kg).

LS3 or *"BigDog"*

BigDog can carry 330 pounds (150 kg) of gear and can run up to 6 miles per hour (10 kph). It is programmed to go over hills, across rubble, and in snow, mud, and water. BigDog's problem is that it runs on a loud gasoline-powered engine. It must be quieter if it is to be used by the military. LS3 could go where vehicles can't, and lessen the weight of soldiers' packs.

XTREME FACT – U.S. Marines tested LS3 or "BigDog" in Hawaii in 2014. It could one day be used to carry heavy supplies such as food and water.

Fish Robots

People love the beauty of fish, but many don't want to take care of them. To solve this, AIRO, a company in Korea, created robot fish. Called MIRO, each fish has a jointed front and back half. Each half has its own motor. This lets MIRO swim like a real fish. The robot fish has LED eyes. Its four sensors allow it to move around objects in its way. MIRO can swim up, down, left, and right. It can be directed with a remote control or swim by itself, autonomously.

MIRO fish can have any "skin" coloring.

XTREME FACT – There are several sizes of MIRO. The biggest is MIRO-9. It is 21 inches (53 cm) long and weighs 5.7 pounds (2.6 kg). It can swim as deep as 16 feet (5 m) and can go for up to 16 hours before needing to recharge.

AquaJellies are underwater robots that mimic the movements of real ocean-living jellyfish. Created by Festo of Germany, AquaJelly is made of three parts. The misty, bowl-shaped top holds the control board and radio sensors. The watertight body contains the batteries and an electrical drive unit that moves up and down, propelling AquaJelly through the water. Finally, it has eight tentacles with fin-like ends. These move in a gentle wave-like motion to help direct its movement. A human-operated computer controls AquaJelly's movements, but it also runs autonomously to keep it from bumping into other AquaJellies.

XTREME FACT – AquaJelly can operate independently. The programming also allows a group of AquaJellies to "talk" and work together as a swarm. They can solve problems through cooperation.

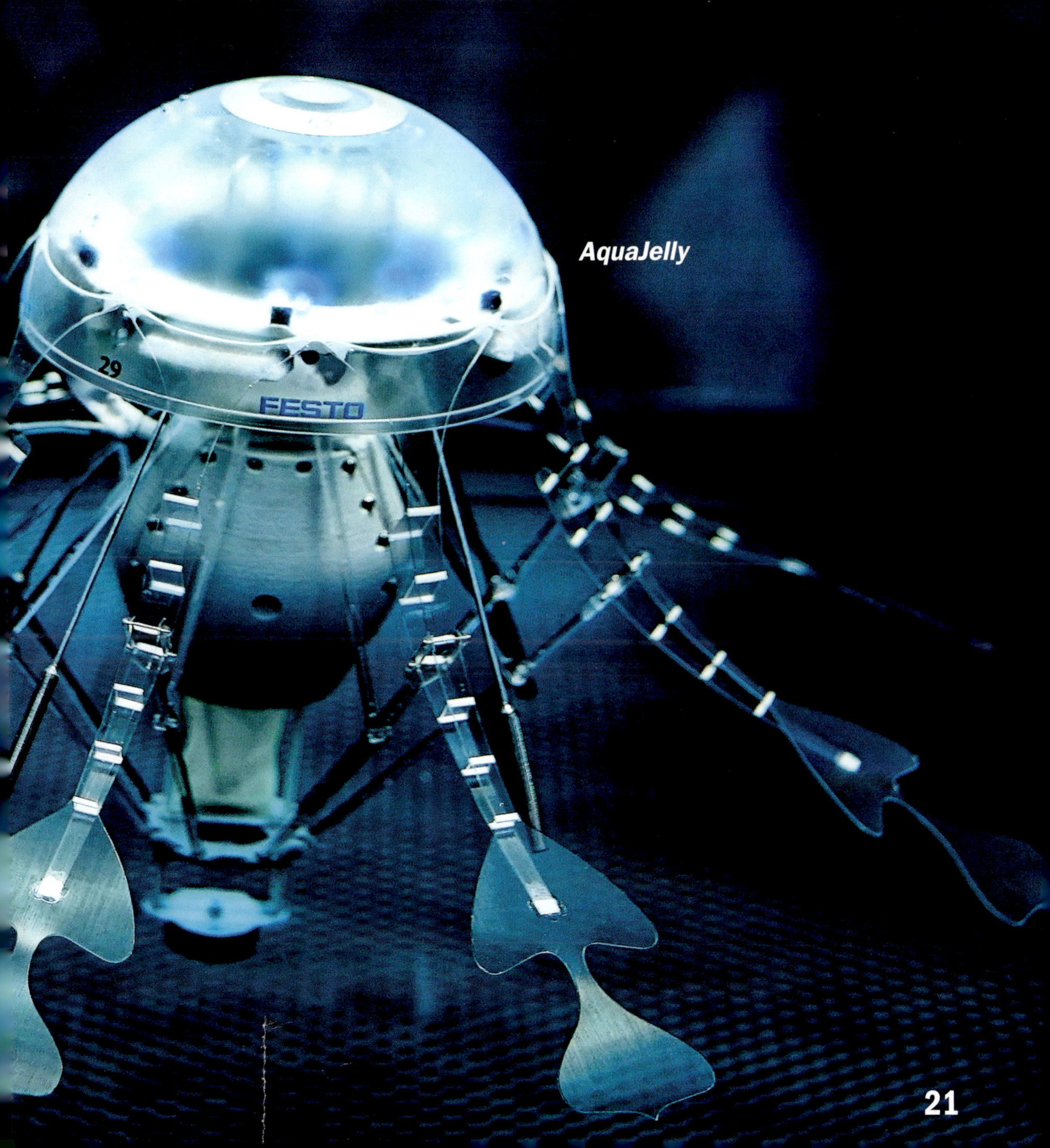

AquaJelly

Bird Robots

Festo's SmartBird is a robot gull with a brain. It looks very much like a real bird as it soars, turns, and flaps its wings. To become airborne, engineers made this robot bird very lightweight. Although it has a large wingspan of about 6.5 feet (2 m), SmartBird weighs about a pound (450 g). It can fly at a speed of 15.5 miles per hour (25 kph) for 20 minutes on one battery charge.

SmartBird

AeroVironment's tiny Hummingbird Nano Air Vehicle (NAV) looks like a real hummingbird. It is about 6 inches (15 cm) long and has a wingspan of 6.3 inches (16 cm). The Hummingbird even makes a "hum" noise when flying. Its wings flap at an incredible speed, allowing it to move up, down, left, and right at up to 11 miles per hour (18 kph). It can even hover in place. Inside the bird is a small video camera. What it sees can be recorded. Could this robotic bird become a spy? It's possible.

The Hummingbird Nano Air Vehicle weighs 19 grams, or less than an ounce. That's about the same as a small mouse.

Spider Robots

Spider robots mimic the talents of real-life arachnids. Vincross's Hexa is a 6-legged, 20-inch (51-cm) -wide spider-like robot. It is equipped with sensors and a spinning camera head with night vision. Human operators control Hexa. It can move forward and back, side to side, or climb stairs. It can even understand hand gestures and colors. What makes this robot unique is that anyone can create programs for Hexa. This is called an "open platform." Amateur and professional roboticists help make Hexa even more amazing.

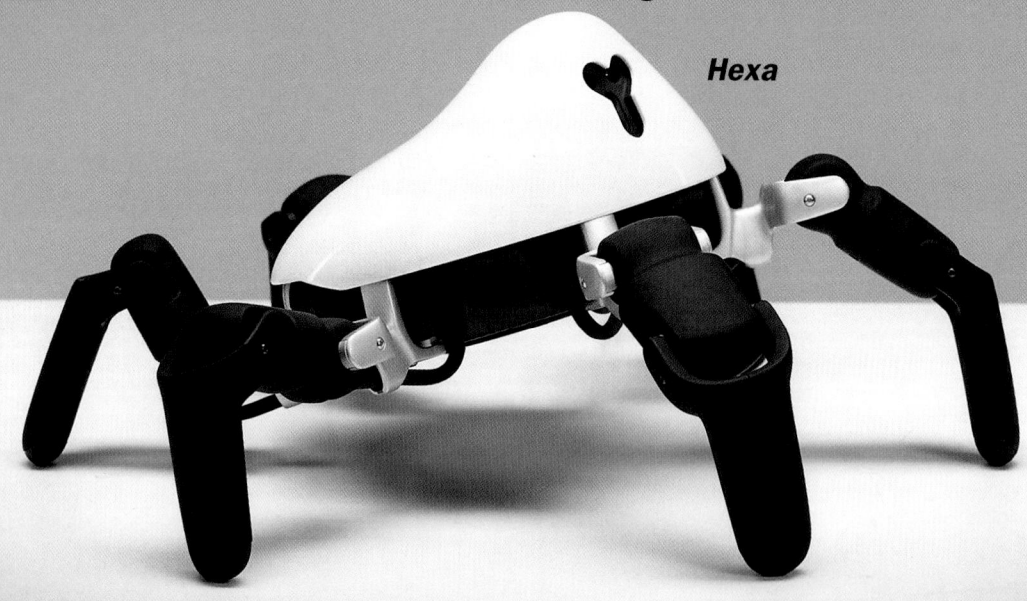

Hexa

A flic-flac spider moves by walking, as well as flinging itself forward in an airborne somersault motion. Festo's BionicWheelBot moves in the same manner. The robotic spider has springs mounted inside its legs. It keeps three legs on the ground and three in the air when walking. Its other two legs stay ready to help it push off, if needed. This lets BionicWheelBot move across rugged terrain.

XTREME FACT – BionicWheelBot can form its legs into a circle and roll for increased speed. Its legs protect its computers, so even if it drops off something as high as a table, it's OK.

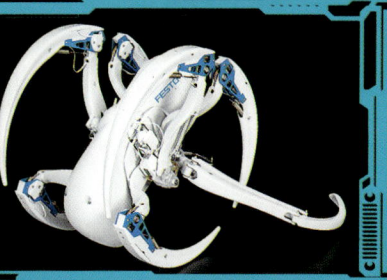

BionicWheelBot

Insect Robots

Festo's BionicANTs work together to do what a single one cannot. ANT stands for Autonomous Networking Technologies. One robotic insect may be tasked with trying to move a heavy object. When it can't do it alone, it signals other BionicANTs for help. ANTs do this autonomously. No central computer or human help is needed.

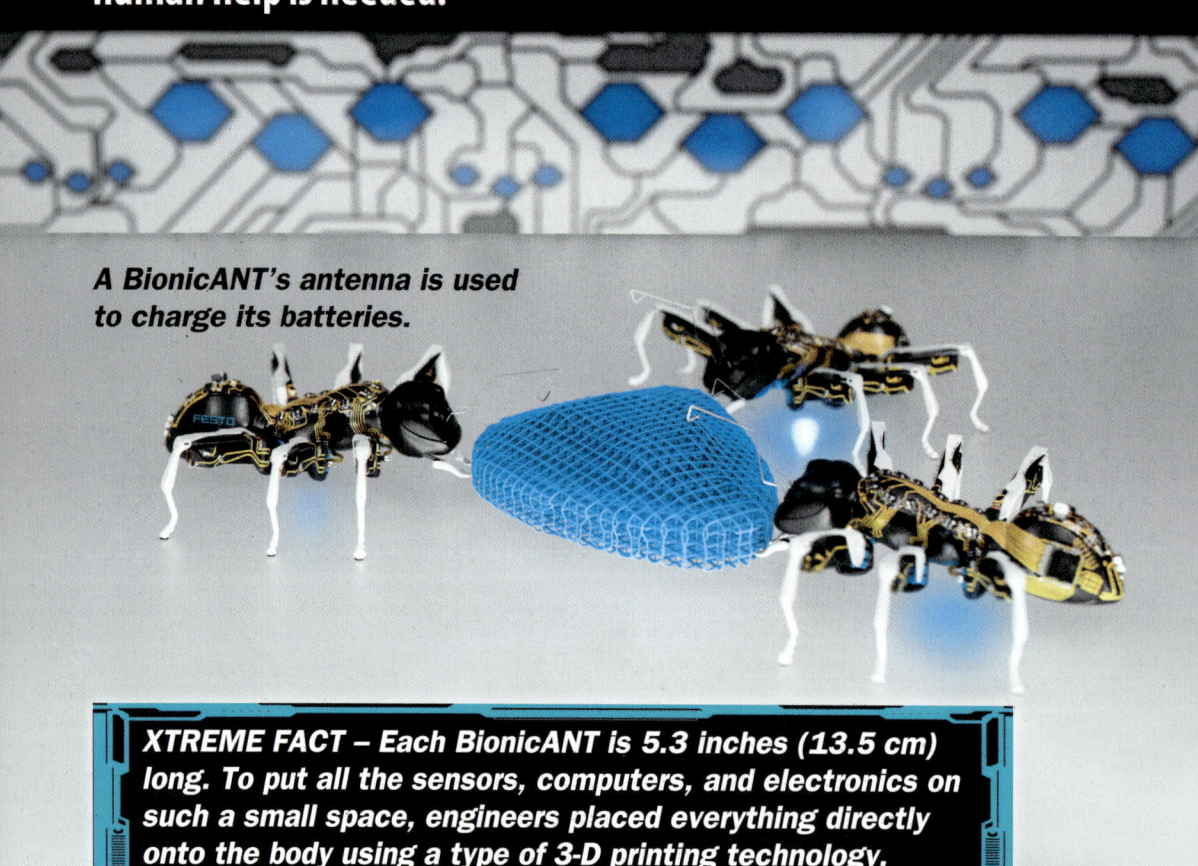

A BionicANT's antenna is used to charge its batteries.

XTREME FACT – Each BionicANT is 5.3 inches (13.5 cm) long. To put all the sensors, computers, and electronics on such a small space, engineers placed everything directly onto the body using a type of 3-D printing technology.

RoboFly

The University of Washington's Autonomous Insect Robotics Laboratory (AIR Lab) has developed RoboFly. To make the tiny robotic fly, engineers had to create an ultralight circuit that weighed less than a toothpick. They then wanted a way to power and control RoboFly that didn't require a long wire tethered to a device on the ground. A small solar cell was attached to the body. When an infrared laser beam strikes it, RoboFly gets the power it needs to flap its wings and become airborne. It has only flown a short distance so far. Ideas are being developed where a ceiling- or vehicle-mounted laser could automatically follow RoboFly and power it constantly.

Amphibian Robots

Pleurobot is a salamander-like robot that can both walk *and* swim. To create this biorobot, engineers from the Swiss company EPFL studied the sharp-ribbed newt (*Pleurodeles waltl*). Pleurobot was made to help learn about spinal columns. It may also be used for search and rescue. It has a camera in its head. It could walk or swim into flooded or dry areas looking for people in trouble.

Pleurobot is 8.6 times bigger than its living counterpart. This was necessary so the robot's body and computer parts could be bigger.

A robot could help doctors see inside a patient's stomach.

A robot that mimics a tree frog's footpads would hold on even in wet conditions.

It does not look like a frog, but the University of Leeds researchers are working on a surgical robot based on the footpads of a tree frog. Stomach surgery is tricky. Doctors need all the information they can get. A tiny camera-wielding robot could use the unique design of a tree frog's footpads to cling to a wet stomach wall. The grip would allow the robotic "frog" to move all around a patient's slippery insides. The clinging robot could even move upside down and vertically, helping surgeons see what's wrong inside a stomach.

Glossary

BionicFlyingFox

ARACHNIDS
A class of living things that includes spiders and scorpions.

AUTONOMOUS
Able to work on its own. An autonomous robot does not have a human operator. Its programming allows it to do its job without help.

BLIND LOCOMOTION
For robots, the ability to use sensors instead of cameras to move.

ENGINEER
A person whose job is to use scientific knowledge to create and maintain mechanical and electronic objects and structures. This includes such things as robots, cameras, and engines.

MIMIC
To do something the same way as something or someone else does it. Animal robots mimic the actions of their living counterparts.

OPEN PLATFORM
When the physical designs or "hardware" of a robot is made public so anyone can look at it and create a software program to make the robot perform a specific task. This is also called "open source."

PROGRAMMING
In robots, a language of coded commands and instructions that allow it to perform specific tasks.

Quadruped
Something with four feet, such as dogs, cats, and mules. Several animal robots are quadrupedal or four-footed.

Sensors
In robots, devices that send out signals and get information from a surrounding area. The robot's computers may use the data to decide what the robot should do next, or pass the collected information on to a human operator.

Spinal Column
The spine or backbone. These small bones run down the back and are connected by muscles.

Tether
A connecting rope or wire. In robots, it may be used to keep an object from moving too far away or as a way to get power to the robot.

Touch-Sensitive
Something that works when a person touches it. Some robots are touch-sensitive, such as robot cats that purr when petted or stroked.

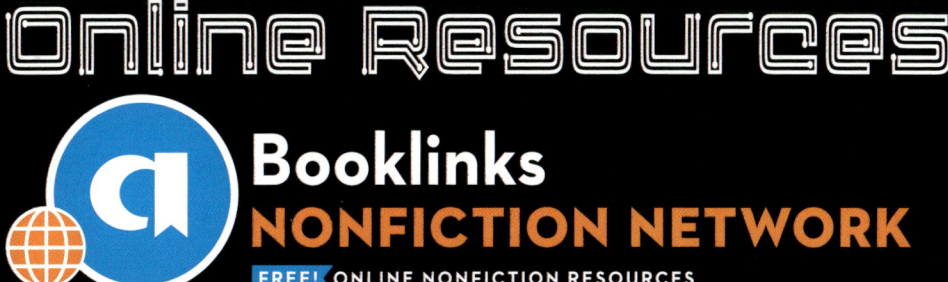

To learn more about animal robots, visit abdobooklinks.com. These links are routinely monitored and updated to provide the most current information available.

Index

A
AeroVironment 23
Aibo 8, 9
AIRO 18
AquaJelly 20, 21
Autonomous Insect Robotics Laboratory (AIR Lab) 27
Autonomous Networking Technologies (ANT) 26

B
BigDog (*see also* LS3) 16, 17
BionicANT 26
BionicFlyingFox 30
BionicWheelBot 25
Boston Dynamics 6, 12, 16

C
Cheetah 14, 32

E
EPFL (company) 28

F
Festo 20, 22, 25, 26

G
Germany 20

H
Hawaii 17
Hexa 24
Hummingbird Nano Air Vehicle (NAV) 23

J
Japan 10
Joy For All 15

K
Korea 18

L
LS3 (Legged Squad Support System) (*see also* BigDog) 16, 17

M
Marines, U.S. 17
Massachusetts Institute of Technology (MIT) 14
MIRO 18, 19
MIRO-9 19

N
Nano Air Vehicle (NAV) 23

P
Pleurobot 28
Pleurodeles waltl (*see also* sharp-ribbed newt) 28

Q
Qoobo 15

R
RoboFly 27

S
sharp-ribbed newt (*see also Pleurodeles waltl*) 28
SmartBird 22
Sony 8, 9
SpotMini 6, 7
Super Monster Wolf 10, 11

U
University of Washington 27
University of Leeds 29

V
Vincross 24

W
WildCat 12, 13

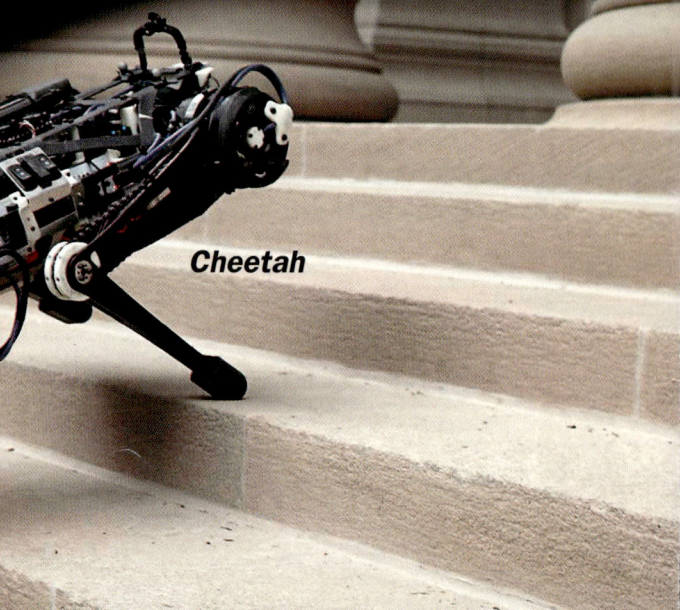

Cheetah

32